Introduction

Failure is inevitable. We all know that.
We learn this fact of life at very young
ages and we develop a response to
failure that often follows us into
adulthood. Most of us learn to adjust
our behavior in order to not experience
failure, or at least, not the kind of
failure that is very obvious or painful.
We attempt ➜ We Fail ➜ We never try
again. The End.
On some level, we all know that the
above pattern is a natural but entirely
juvenile progression. As we develop
and grow, we learn to push back on
our knee-jerk, immature response to
failure. We have countless sayings to
describe this:

"No pain, no gain."
"It has to get worse before it gets better."
"What doesn't kill you makes you stronger."
"If you want the rainbow, you have to put up with the rain."
And yet.
If we are brutally honest with ourselves, the degree to which we have internalized this reality is not extreme. We set the bar low. We excuse our choices with equally famous phrases like "I'm only human" and "I can only do so much." Or, we camouflage our choices to not try (risking failure) as choosing balance or contentment...in Humans may be at their most creative when they are trying to justify their own mediocrity.

How often do we unthinkingly change our behavior in order to not experience failure? Put another way, how much and how often do we not try just so we don't fail? If you're reading this, you have to be breathing and if you are breathing, you are alive and if you are alive, the answer to that question is: MUCH more often than you realize! As evolved as any one of us may be, the magnet-like pull to avoid failure is immeasurably strong and somehow, every day, we give in to it.

If you imagine a typical day in your head, starting at the beginning, it won't take you long to come to the first occurrence of something you do mainly to avoid failure. Take a moment to imagine the best that could happen in that scenario and then choose to start there, adjusting your actions based on possible success instead of the fear of failure. And know this: it may not "work." Failure leads to failure leads to failure...until it doesn't! Success ONLY comes after failure and usually that looks like this: Failure → Failure → Failure → Failure → Failure → Success!

Mediocrity requires no change. Success demands it. The path to growth is a direct route to your own failure...and your own success. You are not a child, you can do this. Be bold: fail successfully!

"It is hard to fail, but it is worse never to have tried to succeed."- by Theodore Roosevelt

CHAPTER 1

Beginning of Failure

I was born in a small town in North Carolina. I saw my mother and father's marriage suffer and end badly because of money problems. I was the only child, so I really didn't understand divorce. And really, my father and my mother couldn't see eye to eye. My dad was known as a stingy man and my mother was a big spender. That caused a conflict in the home. My dad wanted to save every penny and my mom wanted to buy every dress from Cato's. Money wasn't a subject that was talked about around the house that often. It was kind of a forbidden subject. To this day, money is still a subject my mother and father will not discuss with me. No matter how old I am, they still won't discuss money with me. I guess it was a generational thing. I knew at that age I would always discuss money around my kids and my wife. My mother and father were hardworking folks. I mean, they were 60 hours in a week into plans. My mother is retired from 35 years on one job and my dad is still working. I believe he is at 45 years on his job right now. The lesson I learned from my parents is to never quit and pick up one career field and stick to it. The last part of the lesson was my biggest challenge for me. I remember when I wanted to be a business owner. It happened in the 3rd grade. We had a career day and the parents were lined up in the hallway looking down and out. I can't even remember joy coming over their faces. They were in total depression mode. My parents couldn't make it of course because they work all the time. After the parents left the class, our teacher made us write down what we wanted to be when we grew up. Of course, 99% of the class wanted to be what was just presented to them. My answer was to own a big company. My teacher looked at my paper and looked at me, and shook her head. I never asked her what she meant by the head shake. I can only guess that my dreams were kind of too big, I should dream smaller. I ran home from the bus stop to tell my mother and my father the big news. That I was going to own a major corporation one day. When I walked into the home, my mother had the same look on her face of disgust and depression, so I just kept all those dreams and thoughts to myself. My grandfather was the first business owner that I knew. He owned a concrete company. He ran that company until he couldn't do it anymore. He twice and he couldn't stay away. What I learned from him was how to hustle and work extremely hard to own your own company. There were some things I didn't learn by my own fault. My grandfather stayed in his company for over 60 years. It seems like a common theme. My parents and my grandfather stayed on the one career path. If I would've learned this simple principle at an early age, I believe I could have been wealthy in my early 20s. Guess I failed over and over again. My first job came when I was 16 years old. I worked for Bojangles, a chicken fast-food restaurant. They started me at $5.45 an hour. I remember getting my first check realizing, "I need to make more money." My cousin, he worked with me. He needed to make more money also. My internal drive was so big and so profound during those early childhood ages that I was always driven to be the best. I used to look at videos of famous athletes and professional football players, and professional basketball players. And always dreamed of being on that platform so I could make millions. It was never about the love of the game for me, it was always about how much money they made. When I played football, it was all about the cash because money was king. Guys making millions, and now today they make way more than what they would've made back in the days I was looking at football. Emmitt Smith, Dion Sanders was guys I looked up to. Looking at players today like Darrelle Revis, he done made so much money ($40-50 million) playing football. Michael Vick signed $200 million contracts. So football to me was not about the love of the game, it was all about the money, I wanted to make that kind of money. I used to ride around and look at houses when I was a kid, probably the only 18/17-year-old that was riding around neighborhoods looking at big mansions and dreaming of living in these houses and driving, looking at nice cars. That's what I wanted, that's what I was going after. So, I decided to go work at Chic-Fi-La after I left Bojangles. I did that right out of high school and I looked at my check and I was like, "Man, this ain't nothing. I ain't going to get there. This ain't the money I was looking for." So I went to talk to the Chic-Fi-La boss and I asked for a raise. He wouldn't give me a raise. He had other people in there that deserved the raise more than me, I guess. But I wanted to be him. I didn't want to be the assistant manager or a shift leader, I wanted to be the owner of Chic-Fi-La. So I kept asking him questions, "How did you own it? How much money did you need?" All these different things that the average 17 or 18-year-old kid don't really ask for their boss. "How much money does it take to own a Chic-Fi-La. He wouldn't tell me. I guess he didn't think I would ever get there one day. So, I left Chic-Fi-La and I decided to make cash for myself. I wanted daily tips. I wanted to basically hustle and see how good I could hustle, and see how much money I could actually make in a day. So I went right across the street to a car wash called TLC,

CHAPTER 2
Failing at the Hustle

I decided to wash and detail cars. And I began to bring home $100-$150 a day from detailing cars because I was really good at it. Somebody decided to say, "Aye man, you a hustler man. You can make some serious money if you decided to do something else." And I was like, "What? Go ahead and tell me what that something else is!" And he was like, "Man, you ever sold drugs before?" And I was like, "Nah man, my daddy told me not ever do something like that." And he was like, "Man you can make serious money." He also had a High end Mercedes Benz. It like similar to most network marketing companies, they entice you with the nice luxury cars. It didn't take much because

money was my passion. "Yea, I'll do it."
So at 18 years old, I decided to drop my
job and sell drugs as a career. I had a lot of
money and worked in-between New York
and Florida. After the drug dealers decided
they wanted to kill my family, my
grandfather had to get me out of trouble I
owe some serious money to some major
drug dealers in the area. I was risking
everything I put my family in harm's way
just to make a quick buck. After I failed at
selling drugs, I decided to step away and
go into the Marines.

CHAPTER 3

Failing at Service

I went to Boot-Camp, and I treated it also as a business transaction. Everything I do in life is almost like a business transaction. I had a smile on my face the whole time. I felt it was the great place to start my career. While in the Marines I was offered an opportunity to help build a network marketing company. Notice that almost all network marketing companies start or find its way around military bases. It was my first time in this. I got in contact with millionaires. I was shocked! One guy even spoke with me for a whole hour and listened to me, and talked to me about success, He explained to me on how to become wealthy. Stick to an industry and work hard at it. It sounded simple at the time, but it was, in fact, harder than it sounded. I went from selling home phone service, and cable like Dish Network and DirecTV. On my last and worst year in the Marines, I was sent to the Brig for 10 days for disobeying a lawful order. I started drinking heavy, at this time my first marriage had completely fell apart. During my time there, I read books and thought of joining Real Estate. I heard it was the best field to get into. I didn't know anything about it, other than it was something the millionaire had told me in my earlier days in the marines. He said around 75% of the wealthy invest in Real Estate. He said deal with apartment complexes, I remember one 1 that was in my hometown of Fayetteville.

It ranged about 5 million in value. I sent it to the bank for approval and I got a yes! I teamed up with a marketing agent and she became of great help. However, as I was getting ready to buy the apartment complexes, I ended up in jail. I got caught with a business partner infidelity. A girl told a cop that I stole her TV, you know she wasn't even on the lease. You have to be careful of the friends you keep. After about 7 days, I went back to try and settle the deal but the opportunity had passed. Another failure. After leaving the marines, I moved to Jacksonville, North Carolina. I got my Real Estate license and started selling mobile homes. I moved back to Fayetteville, NC and moved back to my house and slept on her couch. My life took a full circle. I thought I was mature and grown man, but in reality I was still a little boy. Sometimes in Business you need to fail in order to be successful and you might have to start over, there is light at the end of the tunnel.

CHAPTER 4

Failing in Sales

I looked up to a guy who sold mobile homes and made around 800,000 a year. He was swindling deals and doing fake loans. He would find a way to evict them. He was a con-artist, and I did not realize this until it was too late. Others told me stories of him as well, so I had to figure a way to get out of working with him. I decided to try and get fired. I took a lady out and showed her what the mobile houses looked like and I got fired. I was ecstatic that he fired me! I didn't want to be a "quitter". Come to find out later the guy got caught in a Ponzi scheme. He stole over 20,000,000 million dollars from investors. I really dodge that bullet!

CHAPTER 5

Failing at Service 2

After that horrible experience, I joined the Army and went back to school for business to broaden my knowledge, on business. They put me in all of the classes that I didn't need, and I ended up getting a call about being deployed to Iraq. During this time, I had just got married to the love of my life and we shared the same perspective. We decided to build on our dreams and our lives. Before I left for Iraq, I suffered from appendicitis. I was being poisoned from my busted appendix. I kept throwing up and passing out and after an emergency check, I had to have it removed or I was going to die. I couldn't trust the Army anymore since they ignored my sickness for their training. I went to Iraq with a unit that I couldn't trust with my life. I read around 100 books that year on leadership and mentorship, we got bombed every night, at some point I decided to just stay in bed instead of running to the bunker. While in Iraq my wife Grandmother was put on life support, I ended up leaving Iraq to be with my wife through our family tragedy.

CHAPTER 6

Failing at Family

My wife's grandmother had passed away from heart failure. It was a traumatic moment in our lives. When I got home on emergency leave, my wife and I decided adopted her brothers and sister. There were 6 kids to be taken care of. I fought to leave the army to take care of my family. I got out the Army on a hardship discharge, it was hard we had no money. I remember trying to get jobs and going to the unemployment office and no one hire me because of the record I received from the Marines, I remember the feeling I had when I had to ask the government to help feed my family, as man I felt like I let my family down, the lesson I learn no matter what don't quit, because I had whole looking to me to be strong. So I went back into detailing cars every day. I need a job to pay every day, not every week, we only made 700 a month and it was hard to keep food on the table. I told my wife I had to go back into the military for the money. But before I did, I decided to do something crazy. I decide to "hustle" again because I felt I was out of options. But you are never out of options, there are plenty of other options that are not illegal. However, I decided to sell as many drugs as possible. The day I was going to get a package of drugs, I got a call from the Army that they was going allow me back in the military I was blessed because I didn't know what was waiting for me at the dealer's pick-up site. I felt like I was being set up by the FEDS. I mean was going sell Kilos. Thank God he answered my wife prayers.

CHAPTER 7
I just Failed

I had to get deployed again to Iraq, and I had to volunteer to support my family. However, I ended up going to Indiana. After praying, our whole unit ended up staying Indiana and our deployment to Iraq got canceled for 2 years. In those 2 years, I wanted to get involved in Real Estate again. So I was looking for properties and talking o lenders. I was making deals happen and learning to make a deal with no money down. I simply just got the knowledge of it. I went back to school and decided to take classes online to speed up the process of getting my degree in business without taking unnecessary classes.

I was looking at different companies to enter. In 2008 I was deployed again, this deployment was my worst time ever in Iraq. I was injured 6 months into the deployment. I lost felling in my legs. After coming home I was medically discharge from the Army. The Army retired me out. At this time I had lost everything. It was about 8 months before I received any benefits from the VA and Social Security, our cars was repo, we were placed on government assistance again. Man I was struggling with this one, I was too hurt to go out and work. After we got our benefits, we decided to move to Austin, TX and buy a house. The kids were graduating and marriages were happening, so the pain in the struggle subsided. I was doing everything I could to accomplish my dream of having a big house and flourishing.

I sat up one night watching an infomercial. I bought what they were offering. What they were offering was illegal in Texas, I didn't realize until 3 years later when I was getting my Real Estate license. After that horrible experiment I decide to get involved with Financial Service Company.

CHAPTER 8

Network Marketing Failure

Here in this chapter I will be telling you some things about network marketing that I feel I expose my family to. This is meant to give you a clear perspective. I hope it helps. Remember earlier in the book I was approach about selling drugs. The things that entice me was the idea of a different lifestyle. Do you notice that network marketing companies target the poor and middle class? What about the wealthy? The reason they don't target the wealthy is because the wealthy don't need the pitch. Can you imagine walking up to a millionaire and ask him if he would like to make an extra 1500 to 2000 a month. Wouldn't the wealthy have more connection than the poor? I totally messed up my family. I would get involve with these companies the training teaches you to reach to your family and friends and even your grandmother to get them into the business. Doing this causes you to alienate your friends and family. It will cause you set up fake cookouts and parties to fool people to come over. I did these things to family members and friends. Even to this day I am trying repair the relationship with my family. My next book will be about Truth Network Marketing. I will outline every network marketing company.

CHAPTER 9

Failure at Real Estate

I went back to school again and got my license in Real Estate and sold houses. I started with a company who was known for the brand, the company model itself off network marketing. I soon left that company and landed at smaller firm, where my skill set was put to test. I was great at getting clients and my business partner was great at closing them. We started a commercial division inside the Real Estate Company. I taught others about Commercial Real Estate. I enjoyed helping people grow. We were on pace to close around 20 million in Real Estate, the problem we had all the clients and no building or locations to place them. After about 6 months of having around 8 clients that list went down to around 4 and then eventually zero. I failed once again. I failed my clients and my business partner and more than anyone else I failed my family again, by not closing the deal. My wife and I decided to move to Dallas and build a Commercial Division. After three months of struggling I decided to try my hand in working with another Financial Services Company. This time I keep it from my wife, because it was just hard to look at my family and see the disappointment on their faces at another failure. I quickly realize I was a glorified salesperson, the trick is when you go into these Financial Services Company they tell you are a business owner and that all you have to is build a team of agents to sell for you. However you really don't own any of the business. Aren't taught in the process of it. I wanted to own my on company with my name on it, something I can leave my kids. Don't get involve in Real Estate or Financial Services thinking you own the company or you a business owner. (YOU ARE NOT)

CHAPTER 9

Failed My Way To Success

I remember I was headed to Vegas for 5 days to a convention, and the night before I left to go on this trip, my wife and I got into heated discussion about my failure and about my life long pursuit of success and how I am not business owner or even worse I not a boss. She really got after me and said your whole life was based on sales and making everyone around you rich. What have that profit you in the past 12 years? I worked 80 hours a week to put money into someone else hand, needless to say I decided to open my own company. I went to Vegas for 5 days and seen around two thousand people run around excited to sell insurance products. I was really thrown off and set right in the convention and built my company and wrote down everything I am great at doing. I landed in Business Consulting and Business Coaching. The reason for this field is very simple I want to share my failures and help other business owners be successful and avoid the pitfalls of failure, I also started an online university called Champion University, it's geared to help young business owner on the journey of ownership. Traditional college has lied to the business owner. They convince the business owner that going back to college and getting a degree in business will automatically teach you how to open a business, but really what that degree get you is 60,000 to 100,000 worth of debt. It turns your passion into owning a business to going and getting a job to pay off the massive debt. What I decided to was take that education platform and teach on the three pillars of Business Ownership. Business, Finances, and Ecommerce (Social Media Marketing). My University is the alternative. Success to me is when my wife says, "you made it", and my kids can look at me and be proud of me. Today, I am content with my success. I will continue to strive, and I hope you do the same. I hope there I san uncovering of my story that will help you develop your story. My integrity, my principle, and success in business I based off of my failures. Zig Ziglar stated, "The more people you help to become wealthy, the wealthier you will be". I realized that the more people I helped, the more it helped me as well.

I failed at a lot of things. However, my failures led to this very book I am writing. When you feel you are losing at certain things in life, you have to put things into perspective. Failing is a part of the process to success. You don't truly fail until you quit. Failing your way to success is a part of life. So don't quit.

CHAPTER 10

20 Question about Success

1 How Do We Win Building Knowledge?

-Appear weak while going strong when you're ready to strike.

You want to soak in all the knowledge; read as many books as possible. You want to plan your life out. Start focusing on daily plans instead of yearly plans. Plan all the ways your business can fail before you even start. You can answer every fail question this way.

-Become a monopoly. In other words, become the only one that can operate in that sector. What happens is in certain companies, people will build the same company in the same neighborhood. For example, there are two security companies in the same neighborhood. They then come together and bridge the gap and become partners so they can monopolize the security industry in that neighborhood/community.

#2 How do you prepare for uncertainty?

- Watch out for mega trends. Anticipate black swans. Mega trends are events that happen in the market place. When the housing market crashes or when it is on the rise, when sales at certain stores collapse or are closing, and when cities make major decisions about their communities that affect the whole neighborhood are mega trends. Mega trends even include voting for presidents, voting for office, and any major decision within your business being made. You also have to watch out for mega trends because they have tests and implications to your business. There are decisions between cutting taxes and saving on taxes. Either way it goes, you want to be able to plan and prepare for uncertainty.

In other words, anticipate black swans. Black swans are major disasters that happen. Like hurricanes and floods. These are things you want be prepared for.

#3 What Will Help You Make Smarter Decisions?

- Read books. Read as many books as possible on the current subject matter. If you are going into landscaping you want to read as many books on landscaping as possible. You have to be self-educated. You do not necessarily have to go to school in this case and pick up a landscaping degree. You learn from self-advocacy and self-knowledge. Read. Read. Read.

#4 What Do We Know About Change?

Change is the hardest thing to accomplish in life, because no one wants to change. Everyone is stuck with their opinion and ideas and no one is open to change. However, the moment you become open to change, the moment you become rich.

#5 What Is The Best Way To Do The Work?

- Hard work is the best way to do you work. When you are going hard at your business, failure becomes easy. When going hard and pushing yourself beyond the limits, failure tends to become part of the process. Push your way to success.

#6 How Can I Possibly Get Everything Done?

- You have to block off your day. Cut your days down into segments. Cut your day down as far as possible; fifteen minute to thirty minute segments. Get on a routine and schedule. The faster you are able to get on a schedule, the faster your day becomes easier. You will be able to see you are able to get everything you need to get done completed in your day. Honey-dew lists will not cut it. They do not account for things that happen on the role. Planning your day in increments will give you the ability to move things around and plan when things do not go according to plan.

#7 What System Should We Use To Track How We Are Doing?

-It is all about analytics. Computer guys use analysts to track how many things they are selling, how their business is going, and what demographics are going on in certain areas. They use analytics, but on a day-to-day basis where computers are not used often, you still need to keep track of your customers and so forth. You need to become the person who takes track of everything and get to know your customers.

8 What Is Our Ideal Organizational Design?

- Your organization should be designed off of what your customer needs. Every business should be based off of the service for the client or customer. You need to build your company based off the service towards others and it grows as others grow. When you see companies that fail, it is because they built it off of the *owner's* idea of the company instead of the customers' needs. Most businesses that are successful build it of their needs. Look at Jerry Jones and the *Dallas Cowboys*. He built the stadium based off of customer wants and needs instead of his own. His stadium became a national monument, where everyone is trying to come and see it. So, build your business off of the design of others' needs.

#9 How Should We Grow?

-You should grow fast. Grow as fast as possible. There is another Mark Zuckerberg sitting in an office somewhere trying to create the next innovative idea. If you feel you have an idea that makes sense and can make money and help you grow and become successful, you need to become the fastest land animal in the world. You need to go cheetah fast.

#10 What Do We Know About Global Expansion?

-You have to expand outside of your comfort zone. Most people do not want to globalize their company because they only think about the customers they serve in their company. But what if they decided to go further with their business and expand it nationwide? The problem with most companies is they stay focused on their community only and never understand globalization and tap into the company's growth. For example, soul food restaurants only cater to people who eat soul food. However, if they were to expand they could be able to create every food in that place. If you were from the Caribbean or even from China, you could eat at that restaurant because they cater to everyone globally.

#11 How Do We Attract Customers?

- Attracting customers is easy when you have the right product. Most of the time we would rather sell the product we personally invent instead of selling the right product. Fast foods such as *McDonald's* and *Burger King* never changed their products, they only changed the combination strategies within their menus. The customers are attracted to the sexy, young company. We live in a generation where young and hip is what is attractive. For example, golf courses do not attract or cater to the younger audience because it is not young and sexy. It is typically for the older and rich guys. However, now they are trying to attract *Puma* and *Nike* brands to attract the younger generation to golf and make it young and hip. That is why Rickie Fowler and Jordan Spieth are so important. They are attractive and in return, making golf attractive.

#12 What Is The Best Way To Motivate?

- The best way to motivate yourself is to always put yourself in the position to where you can be motivated. That means turn the television off! Sometimes you have to turn the reality shows off and sit and listen to good teaching of motivation. Try a motivational DVD, take a motivational trip, or ride through the neighborhood to spark an idea. Look at competition and see what they are doing that may be different from what you are doing.

#13 What Should We Do For Our Employees?

- There are incentive programs that you should put into place, like family vacations. "If you sell this much product, you go on a family vacation with all expenses paid". "If you do this great at work, we shall reward you." This shows the employees that you appreciate what they are doing.

#14 What Is Honorable?

-Honor has something to do with your integrity. How do you maintain integrity in your business? How do you maintain being honorable? In the marines or army, you are discharged with an honorable discharge. This means you have completed your obligation to the country and now they discharge you and you get rewards. If you are discharged with dishonorable discharge then you do not get to reap the benefits or rewards. You do not want to waste four years and get a dishonorable discharge while the person next to you gets honorable and reaps all of the benefits. So the same with your business. If honorable, you reap all benefits in growth. If dishonorable there is no growth.

15 How Can We Fulfill Our Potential?

- Potential is based off your level of confidence. So if the level of confidence in your business is great then the potential is magnified. There is no potential without confidence. Confidence breathes potential and you become a super star in your sector. You become LeBron James of your sector. You become Kobe Bryant and Michael Jordan, the greatest of all time.

#16 How Can I Work And Still Be Me?

- Sometimes we take on the brand of our company. We start to wear our company every day. and that is where you have to measure your life out to where you don't carry your company everywhere you go. You need to leave your company in places to grow on its own. You shouldn't become your company and your company shouldn't become you. Your company should instead be an extension of who you are, not all of who you are. You should be an extension of your company. If something were to happen to you, your company should be able to survive without you being there. That is how great your company should work and you can still be you.

-#17 Why Does a Business Expertise Exist?

-Simply put, it is created to give you the best possible situations to win. We live in a country where winning is not the main source anymore, where everyone gets first place votes. Winning is not the only thing that matters anymore since everyone wins. When you create an atmosphere where everyone wins, everyone loses. You have to create an atmosphere at a company where it sets itself to where you are going to win. You are going to have to do whatever it takes to win. Winning is all that matters. Kobe Bryant and Michael Jordan were great because of their competitive nature. Tiger Woods was great as well. They were all great because they wanted one thing. They wanted to win.

#18 What the Hell is Leadership?

Leadership is the example you set in a company, no matter what happens if it fail than I failed as a leader. If the least person in the company can't grasp the concepts than I failed as a leader. The reason why most business failed is the leader or CEO of the company only cares about the top 1% of the company. When a company don't care about the bottom tier of the company than you failed as a leader. The CEO should have training in place that teaches the bottom employee on How to Become the CEO. With these training in place, will cause the lower tier employees to CEO their section. Means this will cause them to act like the CEO in their sector, they will develop CEO responsibility.

19 Who is the Best Business Owners?

If you own the company and you never take time over from work or vacation with your family, it is time to hire a CEO. The best owner of a company has hired a CEO or General Manager to run the company while Im absent. The best owners actually are those who buy their time back. Buying time back means work hard for a short period of time, sacrifice your free time. The reward for the sacrifice is your Time.

#20 How do the Business World Work?

The business world works in a capitalism world, free enterprise world. We have become a socialistic society. That means we are started to be totally dependent on the government for every aspect of our lives. We are becoming a warfare nation. Socialism is when the money that the wealthy get is equally disturbed among the poor. That means there is no class of people anymore. We are all equal. Our income has become equal. When we give capitalism up, we are the mercy of the government. They will control where you eat at, cars you drive and where you live at. We have to fight for free enterprise for the sake of our kids. We need more business owners in the Marketplace, so we want lose control to make as much money we want, and live where we want.

This book was written out of the pain and failures in my life and business and hope you learned that true success can only be obtain through the failure in life and business.

Dante Gibson

Dante Gibson Consultants is a company that helps with startups and existence business owner who maybe at the crossroads of failing and success. We come and give you a quick evaluation of your company. We will analysis your company from the bottom to the top.

Champion University was founded on the principles on Empowering Entrepreneurs, Education, Execution and Championing Networks & Net Worth's. The Three Champion Mastermind Coaches, Dante Gibson, Travis Patterson, and Wes Brown have engineered an online entrepreneur academy for people who seek greatness, intense training/development and dominating trade secrets from working industry leaders.

www.ingramcontent.com/pod-product-compliance
Lightning Source LLC
Chambersburg PA
CBHW021441170526
45164CB00001B/334